Thoughts to Think By

205 Deep Thoughts from the Shallow End

by
Mark A. Kwasny

Thoughts to Think By: 205 Deep Thoughts from the Shallow End

Requests for permission or further information should be
addressed to mark@markkwasny.com.

Printed in the United States of America

ISBN-13: 978-0-9849603-2-3
ISBN-10: 0984960325

To Francis, who did everything but the typing.

ACKNOWLEDGMENTS

This book was inspired by Greg Smrdel who made the mistake of saying something dumb like, "If I can write and publish a book, then anyone can."

THOUGHTS TO THINK BY

205 DEEP THOUGHTS FROM THE SHALLOW END

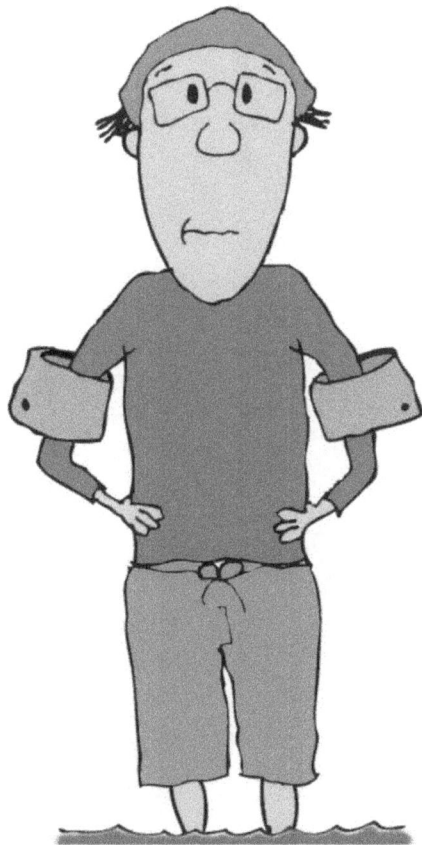

MARK A. KWASNY

It isn't a good idea to try and sweep all your troubles under a rug. For a job that big, you should consider using a shop vac.

If people think you're the biggest loser they've ever met, just remember... that makes you a winner.

If you insist on taking life's challenges head first, at least wear a helmet... and probably a chest protector.

Seeing your glass as half-full doesn't make you a pessimist. Instead, it should make you angry at the bartender for not filling your glass to the top.

When the door of opportunity won't open, crawl in through the window. Then have a good story to tell the police when they arrest you for breaking and entering.

Today is a great day to tell your neighbor you love him. Then, when he's not looking, return the weed whacker you borrowed from him last June.

I was happy to hear the TSA finally caught some terrorists: A group of circus clowns from Missouri. They've been terrorizing children for years.

I think it's a pretty sure sign you've given up on life when you buy cheap toilet paper.

They say 40 is the new 20, until you try to bend down and pick something up off the floor.

Driving in the HOV lane while you're talking to yourself -- or imaginary friends -- doesn't count as having two or more people in the car.

Some people say dogs go to Heaven. But it sure isn't Heaven for the unlucky guy whose job it is to clean up after them.

Whenever a company tells you they're a 'green business,' make sure it's not because they have an uncontrollable mold problem.

If you ever go missing and your face turns up on a milk carton, your family may never know you're gone if they don't drink milk.

With everyone going organic these days, it makes you wonder why there are still so many people who are loaded with artificial fillers, colors, and preservatives.

E ven if you have no convictions, always be on the lookout for a good protest to march in because it still beats having to go into work.

A good way to get rid of an annoying person is to tell a knock-knock joke like, "Knock, knock." "Who's there?" "The IRS."

Drinking a few cups of coffee in the afternoon may wake you up, but remember... coffee wakes up idiots too.

If you step on your bathroom scale and it tries to charge you for excess baggage, it may be time for a new scale. Or a new diet. Or a new psychiatrist.

You might think you're pretty smart with your advanced degree, working in a cubicle. But keep in mind that the janitor always gets his own office.

Everyone says killing two birds with one stone is a great strategy for success. But boy, do they ever change their tune when the birds are bald eagles.

They say that dogs are man's best friend, but for a forever pet, consider a pet rock. They never die.

People who scream at you for being intolerant are usually people no one can tolerate being around in the first place.

You may not like to think about it, but when you go shopping for a new vacuum cleaner, you're looking for the one that sucks the most.

A good way to keep from losing your mind is to not allow it to wander off by itself in the first place.

One way to make 1-D people more interesting is to wear 3-D glasses.

Switching your car insurance to 'No Insurance' is a great way to save 100% on your car insurance bill.

It's true you can never go home again, especially if your family moves out and doesn't tell you.

One way to deal with a narcissist is to admire her clothing, then ask her how much she paid for it at the thrift store.

Why do people who don't like to be told
what to do use GPS?

Of all the people who walk out of your life, make sure the garbage man isn't one of them.

When it's 'Bring Your Kids to Work Day' at the Darwin Institute of Evolutionary Studies, people get upset when you call their kids 'monkey boy' and 'fish face.'

If you ever want to silence the voices in your head, make it a point to not laugh at their jokes. It hurts their feelings.

You know your self-esteem has hit rock bottom when you allow your magazine subscriptions to lapse just so you can get those 'We want you back!' renewal notices in the mail.

Beware of women who wear revealing tops. You never know if it's an invitation or a cry for help.

Don't count yourself as anything special until someone has a bobble head made that looks like you.

If you ever find yourself enjoying a warm, crackling fire in your living room, make sure it's because you have a fireplace.

One of the biggest challenges of taking the road less traveled is that there aren't nearly enough rest stops along the way.

Dogs are God's way of saying 'Sorry' for creating cats.

You know your shirts are really sad when you go to your closet and discover that they hung themselves.

It's a good thing to be unique, just not in a police lineup.

If God was the captain of a kickball team, I'd want to be on His team because, you know, God doesn't lose.

Wrapping yourself in bubble wrap may protect you from car accidents and falls from tall buildings or even from meteor showers. But it won't protect you from people who like to pop bubble wrap.

If you shoot yourself in the head with a water gun, would it be considered attempted suicide or brain washing?

It's really sad when you realize you're going nowhere in life. It's even sadder when you suddenly arrive.

If you ever find yourself on fire, don't run because that will make the fire burn faster. Instead, stay perfectly still until the fire burns itself out.

If your friend tells you she missed you, don't stand so far away from the curb and maybe next time, she won't.

Do you think vegetarians see the irony of cutting their vegetables with a steak knife?

If you're going to be a clown, be a happy, joyful clown. We have enough homicidal maniac clowns in the world already.

If an atheist tells you he doesn't believe in God, tell him you don't believe in gravity. Just don't push him off a cliff to try and prove your point because then you'd both be wrong.

Always look on the bright side, unless a nuclear bomb goes off. Then you should probably look away.

Try to be humble at work because if anyone asks you, "Who died and made you the boss?" you'll have to decide whether or not to show them where the body is.

If you don't bring any vowels to a war of words, you may not win the war, but you may win a few battles for originality.

If you go to unlock your car with the remote button and instead of your car unlocking, the neighbor's cat explodes, you probably hit the wrong button.

If your life is filled with trouble, a good start on the road to recovery is realizing that the one thing all your troubles have in common is you.

If you ever lose your mind, you may have to consider the frightening possibility that it simply decided to run away from home.

It's bad advice to tie a pork chop around your neck to get the dog to play with you, especially if the dog is in a burying mood.

There are so many stupid people in the world that it won't be long before smart people will be able to get handicapped parking stickers for their cars.

There's nothing more annoying than spending all day making paper copies of all your paperless transactions.

Don't feel bad if you don't have a significant other. Instead, enjoy the insignificant others in your life.

The reason people in hell aren't allowed to have social media accounts is because everyone got tired of 'You know it's hot when...' posts.

You know you've hit rock bottom when a
    homeless person hands you his EBT card.

Imitation is the highest form of flattery, except when you get caught copying off your friend's test paper.

Never trust your next bungee jump to a company that boasts of being a premium wireless provider.

Probably the worst place in the world to work is the Weebles factory. Management always expects you to get right back up if you ever fall down.

Everyone tells you that you need to learn how to handle life's ups and downs, but no one ever tells you how to handle life's sideways.

You may think that licking the knife after you make a peanut butter and jelly sandwich is perfectly acceptable, but the person who gets the sandwich probably doesn't think so.

Today is the first day of the rest of your life because yesterday was just a test run.

I think a good way to reply to someone who says, "Don't hate me because I'm beautiful" is, "Don't worry, I won't."

Every man thinks that dating a model is a great thing, but truth be told, most men would rather date a real woman.

When your heart skips a beat, don't assume it's love. Maybe your pacemaker needs a new battery.

There are probably better ways to motivate someone before their shift in the emergency room than, 'Go knock'em dead!'

It should be a crime if you put your breathable cotton shirts in the wash machine and they drown.

If you're going to invest in a money tree, be sure it doesn't come from the Charlie Brown Nursery.

Death is God's way of telling you to get off Facebook.

L ife is short... don't wait for a special occasion to use the sandwich bags with the zipper top.

There's nothing more stressful than discovering the surprise drug test doesn't consist of multiple-choice questions.

Why is it that you can be late for work but you're always right on time for the traffic jam?

Depression is such a negative term. Instead, when you're feeling blue, think of yourself as backwards happy.

If you meet a happy person with a spark in their eye, you can be pretty sure they'll never get a job at the natural gas company.

Getting an envelope in the mail that reads: 'Congratulations! You have been selected from millions' is pretty exciting, unless it's from the IRS.

If you've always wanted to be in a parade, just drive behind the car driving ten miles per hour under the speed limit.

It hurts being called 'intolerant' even though you love milk.

You may think you have a really good self-image, but the mirror may not think so.

There are a lot of people who've never fallen in love, but they sure have stepped in it several times.

People with only one foot never have to experience the frustration of putting both feet in the same hole in their underwear.

A good way to know if your computer has a virus is if the mouse sneezes.

If you ever go into a hobophobic rant down at the rail yard, don't expect those guys to let you anywhere near their box cars.

You'll never understand why no one plays the electric triangle in the school band until you try plugging one in.

If you're having trouble making friends online, make sure the people you are 'CTRL+S'ing aren't 'CTRL+X'ing you.

Before you take a leap of faith, get a brand new pair of shoes. The kind that help you run faster too.

I'll bet it's pretty embarrassing if you're a superhero and you can't go save someone because your uniform is still in the wash machine on 'Spin.'

It's probably not a bad idea to have your car fixed since there are way too many cars on the road already.

If someone compliments you on the nice fragrance you're wearing but you're not wearing any, check to see if the dryer sheet is still clinging to your shirt.

If you don't like the way your life is going, consider going to the dog pound to see if someone will adopt you.

If a bully draws a line in the sand and dares you to cross it, make sure you don't laugh at him if the line is crooked.

The key to being a good multi-tasker is to do one task at a time.

Although some people prefer to look for silver linings in the clouds, I think you're better off just getting cash from the bank.

People should stop hoping for happy endings and instead, focus on happy middles.

D on't be too quick to brag about killing time. It always comes back from the dead with a vengeance.

Are you supposed to be grateful if you lose your gratitude journal?

Today may be a brand new day, but you may want to hold on to the receipt just in case.

They always tell you not to drive your car through standing water. But what if the water is sitting?

A journey of a thousand miles may begin with a single step, but consider taking the bus. Sure beats walking and it's faster too.

Is there a way to tell the live dust bunnies in your home from the dead ones?

If you ever get arrested for running a laundering operation from your basement, be sure to get your clothes out of the dryer before the police take it.

Mocking birds can dish it out, but they sure can't take it.

Power in the wrong hands is a dangerous thing, like the gas station attendant who's in charge of the restroom key.

You know you're following people too closely on Twitter when you get a restraining order.

Probably the most challenging kind of karaoke at the pub is Beethoven night.

A good way to make sure your invitation to the Labor Day party doesn't get lost in the mail is to make sure the hospital has your correct address.

Is there a universal measurement you can point to when someone says, 'How stupid do you think I am?' I think it would be helpful if you could pull out a chart and show people.

When a co-worker dies, it's bad form if you're the first person to help yourself to the staples and rubber bands on their desk. Instead, try to show up second.

Never give your phone number to someone you're attracted to in the grocery store checkout line. They'll just use it to get your reward points.

Never buy a used goldfish. They usually come with a lot of emotional baggage.

There's nothing unusual about your feet falling asleep. But it sure gets creepy when they start sleep walking.

If someone tells you you're never fully dressed without a smile, be careful they don't have you arrested for indecent exposure.

All people are beautiful... except for the ugly ones.

If you get married to the girl of your dreams, don't be surprised if she's gone when you wake up.

A good way to motivate yourself is to believe that nothing is impossible if you lower your standards enough.

People try to cheer you up by saying you shouldn't cry over spilt milk, but tip their beer over once and they'll cry like babies.

It's a sure sign the bum on the street is running a scam when you offer a penny for her thoughts and she says she'll wait for a better offer.

What's the point of spending all that money on life insurance if it's only paid out after you're dead?

If you're sad because you can't find the love of your life, just remember there are plenty of fish in the sea... including a lot of bottom feeders.

If you really want to help the environment, be sure to plant your artificial Christmas tree outside after the season ends.

M ost people like buying stuff. They just don't like paying for it.

If you're looking to make some good money, consider taking a course in speech writing for mimes.

If you're frustrated that you can't predict the future, maybe start out by trying to predict the past and go from there.

People like to excuse their bad habits by saying, "God isn't finished with me yet." But the rest of us wish the construction would go a lot faster.

If money can't buy you love, then why do all the dating sites ask for your credit card information?

The reason people don't like to re-invent themselves is because they're afraid the patent office will reject their application.

There's nothing worse than working with people who scored zero on their personality test.

I f you ever get frustrated by the fact that you can't run away from your fears, try hopping on a plane.

If you decide to donate your body to science, make sure you get a receipt so you can write it off on your taxes.

If you're in the habit of dropping zeros, then a career in accounting probably isn't for you.

There's nothing quite as disappointing as going to the bank and getting two $5 bills instead of two twenties when you ask for change for a ten.

As Thanksgiving approaches, people like to joke about turkeys hiding so they don't become dinner. But you'll never have that problem with Spam.

The one place you don't want to be caught dressed up like a ninja is at a ninja school because they can figure out you're not a ninja real quick.

Sliding down the corporate ladder is much faster and easier than trying to climb up, especially if you're afraid of heights.

On a hot day, it's probably a good idea to stay far away from people who sweat bullets.

Women always want men to be more open and honest. Just not with them.

If your psychiatrist says your problems are all a figment of your imagination, then it's okay to pretend to pay her.

If winning the lottery isn't part of your financial planning, then you shouldn't be surprised if you have to work the rest of your life.

You can bet the animal control people hate it when it rains cats and dogs.

Don't be so smug about knocking off an entire box of Cheerios in one sitting. Getting charged as a cereal killer is no laughing matter.

You may think you're not a materialistic person, but when it comes to clothes, the more material, the better.

Before you go all gung-ho on building abs of steel, maybe you should lower your sights and shoot for abs of aluminum foil first.

If you're going to be an atheist, be a God-fearing atheist. That way, you can probably finagle some vacation time around Christmas and Easter.

If it weren't for nightmares, some people would have no dreams at all.

When you buy someone a thinking cap as a gift, be sure to include batteries. Preferably the rechargeable kind.

Never sneak up on skunks, porcupines, or the guy using a chain saw.

You can tell you're getting old when your favorite ride at the amusement park is the bathroom.

If the company EEO officer tapes mistletoe over the door, don't fall for it... it's a trap.

While it's true that strangers can be friends we haven't met yet, it's not something you want to hear from the creepy guy driving around the neighborhood in the white van.

Happiness is an inside job, but so are indigestion and heartburn.

If your coworkers ever go to the boss's office to accuse you of eavesdropping, be sure to bug the office so you can hear the whole conversation.

When you aim high and shoot for the stars, shoot the closest one because those things are heavy and dragging it home isn't as easy as you might think.

It might be worth a try to sue the manufacturer of your white noise machine for racial discrimination.

If you're afraid you're about to be laid off, file for divorce from the company first, demanding your salary for life and custody of the company car.

You have to be really creative to call in dead to get a day off from work, but not nearly as creative as you have to be to return.

It can be really humiliating to go to a family gathering and be told to sit at the kids' table, especially when your mom snaps your high chair tray on too tight.

One way to tell for sure if your goldfish is dead is to flush it down the toilet and see if it yells for help.

The difference between 'speed' dating and 'Speedo' dating is just one letter, but the psychological damage can last a lifetime.

If you're feeling really down all the time, you may be having an allergic reaction to gravity.

One way to make window shopping at the mall more fun is to do it from your car.

The sounds of nature can be very relaxing, especially the sound of lightning.

You know your computer is taking on a life of its own when you find mouse droppings on your mouse pad.

If you upset a mime, it's possible he'll never speak to you again.

It's always a nice surprise when repair people drop in earlier than expected, except for the roof repair guy.

For the record, the fire department isn't as gentle with you as an adult when you get your tongue stuck to a cold metal pole.

If you get a letter in the mail with one of those 'Forever' stamps on it, be sure to tear it off and use it... forever.

Online relationships: When the only way you can really get along with members of the opposite sex is over vast distances.

Don't be afraid to raise the bar of success. And remember, it's not cheating if you use a stepstool.

If you're going to shoot someone, shoot the messenger. They tell you not to, but someone has to take the fall.

If life hands you a really difficult problem and you can't seem to fix it, try jiggling the handle.

Burning your bridges is rarely a good idea. Instead, use plastic explosives so everything gets destroyed without a trace.

If you go to the grocery store and find that all the labels on the cans have been ripped off, it's a sure sign the terrorists have won.

If you sneeze a lot and there's no one else around, it's safe to assume you're allergic to yourself.

It's quite a thrill to come in first place and win a trophy, but not nearly as thrilling as getting one at a fraction of the cost and effort from the dollar store.

If you're going to kiss anyone at the stroke of midnight on New Year's Eve, I'd suggest you kiss someone from the IRS. You never know when that could come in handy.

Time is not your friend. It's more like a 6'8" mental patient named Ralph who wears a hockey mask and follows you around with a chain saw.

Probably the worst side of the bed to wake up on is the under side.

They say your attitude determines your altitude, but I think it has more to do with the quality of the catapult.

The hardest part about making friends with a shy mermaid is trying to get her to come out of her shell.

So many people worry about the world ending, but I have to tell you, if you run out of toilet paper, your world has already come to an end.

Why is it when people from work go to the bar to make fun of everyone in the office, gripe about the boss, and complain about their job, it's called Happy Hour?

D on't fool yourself into thinking you're living life on the edge if you're still wearing water wings.

If your co-workers ask you to go for a coffee run, don't volunteer unless you're in really good shape.

When it comes to buying flowers for the woman you love, make sure she's not allergic to plastic.

It takes a lot of nerve to ask someone you're attracted to for their number. It takes even more nerve to see if that number works at the ATM.

If fingers could talk and told you where they've been, would your mother let you put them in your mouth?

If you put a penny up to your eye, it can block out the awesome power of the sun. Move that penny a couple of inches up to your forehead and shout, "Hey, look at me... I'm Penny Man!" and you'll look like a total moron.

When you buy a smart car, be sure you don't get one that finished at the bottom of its class.

It's okay if you're not half the man you used to be, but at least shoot for 1/3 or 5/32.

D on't ever try and run away from hard work. Instead, try to avoid it with a good game of hide-and-seek.

Never be afraid to set huge goals for yourself. Then, go find someone brave and strong enough to go get those goals for you.

If the doctor tells you you're too old to have puppies, consider getting a second opinion from another vet.

Political correctness has gotten so out of hand that you're not even allowed to go to a white sale during Black History Month.

It would be really disappointing to come back as a zombie only to discover that brains taste just like chicken.

There's nothing worse than discovering that all your bills are due, especially when you didn't know they were pregnant in the first place.

You may think a movie about your life would be amazing, but chances are, it will never be on the big screen. In fact, it will probably go straight to DVD... in a third-world country.

You know how your friends really feel about you when you discover they've listed you for sale on Ebay.

If your watch dies, don't be surprised if you show up late to its funeral.

If God ever has a garage sale, you should try and go because you can bet He would have some really cool stuff to sell.

How long do fish have to wait to go back into the water after they eat?

If a one-armed man claps in the forest, can anybody hear him?

www.ingramcontent.com/pod-product-compliance
Lightning Source LLC
LaVergne TN
LVHW051049080426
835508LV00019B/1790